Animals All Around

Do Dogs Make Dessert?

A Book About How Animals Help Humans

by Michael Dahl

Illustrated by Jeff Yesh

Special thanks to our advisers for their expertise:

Kathleen E. Hunt, Ph.D.
Research Scientist & Lecturer, Zoology Department
University of Washington, Seattle, Washington

Susan Kesselring, M.A., Literacy Educator
Rosemount-Apple Valley-Eagan (Minnesota) School District

PICTURE WINDOW BOOKS
MINNEAPOLIS, MINNESOTA

D1211698

Managing Editor: Bob Temple
Creative Director: Terri Foley
Editor: Peggy Henrikson
Editorial Adviser: Andrea Cascardi
Copy Editor: Laurie Kahn
Designer: Todd Ouren
Page production: BANTA Digital Group
The illustrations in this book were rendered digitally.

Picture Window Books
5115 Excelsior Boulevard
Suite 232
Minneapolis, MN 55416
1-877-845-8392
www.picturewindowbooks.com

Printed in the United States of America.

Library of Congress Cataloging-in-Publication Data
Dahl, Michael.
Do dogs make dessert? : a book about how animals help humans / by Michael Dahl ;
illustrated by Jeff Yesh.
p. cm. — (Animals all around)
Summary: Introduces a number of different animals and how they help humans.
Includes bibliographical references (p.   ).
ISBN 1-4048-0289-4 (hardcover)
ISBN 1-4048-0378-5 (paperback)
1. Domestic animals—Miscellanea—Juvenile literature.
2. Animals—Miscellanea—Juvenile literature. 3. Zoology,
Economic—Miscellanea—Juvenile literature. [1. Animals—Behavior.]
I. Yesh, Jeff, ill. II. Title.
SF75.5 .D35 2004
636—dc22
2003016528

Do dogs make dessert?

No! Dogs guard people's homes.

Dogs have sharp eyesight, keen hearing, and a good sense of smell. When they sense danger, dogs bark to warn people.

Do honeyguides make dessert?

No! Honeyguides lead people to honey.

Honeyguides fly through African forests, feeding on insects and beeswax. They swoop and chatter, leading humans to beehives. The honeyguides wait for people to open the hives and gather the sweet honey. Then, the birds feast on the beeswax.

Do silkworms make dessert?

No! Silkworms make silk.

Silkworms hatch from moth eggs. They grow, and then they spin soft cocoons around themselves. They spin with silk threads that come from their mouths. One thread can be eight football fields long! People make beautiful clothing from this fine silk.

Do cats make dessert?

No! Cats keep away pests.

Cats are terrific hunters. Farm cats leap and pounce on rats, mice, and bugs. They keep these pests out of barns and silos where grains are stored. Cats also rid people's homes of pests.

Do elephants make dessert?

No! Elephants help clear forests.

Elephants in Asia easily tramp through thick forests and deep swamps. Their heavy heads knock down trees. Their powerful trunks lift logs.

Do horses make dessert?

No! Horses carry people and loads.

Horses can take riders across grassy plains and up mountain trails. They can carry heavy loads on their strong, smooth backs. Sometimes people ride in carts, wagons, or buggies pulled by helpful horses.

Do sheep make dessert?

No! Sheep give people wool.

In the winter, sheep grow shaggy coats of wool. In spring, workers shear the sheep. The wool is cleaned, brushed, and spun into yarn to make blankets, sweaters, mittens, and scarves to keep people warm.

Do water buffalo make dessert?

No! Water buffalo plow wet fields.

Before the sun comes up, water buffalo in Asia are busy working. The heavy creatures trudge through wet, muddy fields. They lower their curved horns as they drag sharp, wooden plows. The plows dig up the soil so the farmers can plant their rice.

Do chickens make dessert?

No! Chickens give people eggs.

Chickens lay eggs every day. Some chickens from Chile lay blue eggs. Some chickens from France lay dark brown eggs. Many chickens in the United States lay bright white eggs. People eat eggs in countless ways for any meal.

Do people make dessert?

Yes! People make dessert.

People make tasty desserts with honey, sugar, and other sweet stuff.
They make puddings and pies. They make cookies and cakes. Yum!
People like to eat dessert.

How Animals Help Humans

Some animals give people things to wear.

silkworms	silk
sheep	wool

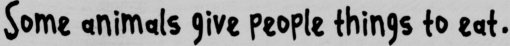

Some animals give people things to eat.

chickens	eggs

Some animals help people work and carry.

honeyguides	lead people to honey
elephants	clear forests
water buffalo	plow wet fields
horses	carry riders and loads

Some animals protect people's homes.

dogs	sense danger
cats	keep away pests

Glossary

Asia—a huge region of the world that contains many countries, including China and India

beehive—a nest or home for bees

beeswax—a yellow substance bees make to create honeycombs where they store honey

buggy—a light carriage pulled by one horse

cocoon—a covering made by a caterpillar to protect itself as it turns into a moth

keen—very strong or sharp. Dogs have keen eyesight and hearing.

pest—an animal that is harmful or bothersome to humans

shear—to cut off with a sharp knife or razor. Sheep ranchers shear the wool off shaggy sheep.

silk—the threads in cocoons spun by silkworms, and the soft, shiny fabric made with those threads

silo—a tall, round tower that stores food for farm animals

wool—the thick, soft coat of a sheep and the yarn made from it

To Learn More

At the Library

Jacobs, Liza. *Water Buffalo*. San Diego: Blackbirch Press, 2003.

McGinty, Alice B. *Guide Dogs: Seeing for People Who Can't*. New York: PowerKids Press, 1999.

Sayre, April Pulley. *If You Should Hear a Honey Guide*. Boston: Houghton Mifflin, 1995.

Schaffer, Donna. *Silkworms*. Mankato, Minn.: Bridgestone Books, 1999.

On the Web

Fact Hound offers a safe, fun way to find Web sites related to this book. All of the sites on Fact Hound have been researched by our staff.
http://www.facthound.com

1. Visit the Fact Hound home page.
2. Enter a search word related to this book, or type in this special code: 1404802894.
3. Click on the FETCH IT button.

Your trusty Fact Hound will fetch the best sites for you!

Index